Plant Parts

Charlotte Lewis

I0807017

ROSEN
COMMON CORE
READERS

Rosen Classroom™

New York

Published in 2013 by The Rosen Publishing Group, Inc.
29 East 21st Street, New York, NY 10010

Copyright © 2013 by The Rosen Publishing Group, Inc.

All rights reserved. No part of this book may be reproduced in any form without permission in writing from the publisher, except by a reviewer.

Book Design: Michael Harmon

Photo Credits: Cover leonello calvetti/Shutterstock.com; p. 4 Adisa/Shutterstock.com; pp. 5, 6 Konstanttin/Shutterstock.com; p. 7 mexrix/Shutterstock.com; p. 8 Dmitry Rukhlenko/Shutterstock.com; p. 9 Katrina Leigh/Shutterstock.com; p. 10 Adam Gryko/Shutterstock.com; p. 11 BestPhotoByMonikaGniot/Shutterstock.com; p. 12 LianeM/Shutterstock.com; p. 13 oksana2010/Shutterstock.com; p. 14 r0ma4/Shutterstock.com.

ISBN: 978-1-4488-8725-5
6-pack ISBN: 978-1-4488-8726-2

Manufactured in the United States of America

CPSIA Compliance Information: Batch #WS12RC: For further information contact Rosen Publishing, New York, New York at 1-800-237-9932.

Word Count: 56

Contents

Plants have leaves.

Leaves get light from the sun.

Plants have stems.

Leaves grow on the stems.

Plants have roots.

Roots get water from the ground.

Some plants have flowers.

Flowers come in many colors.

Some plants have fruit. The fruit grows from the flowers.

Fruit has seeds inside of it.

New plants grow from seeds!

The Parts of a Plant

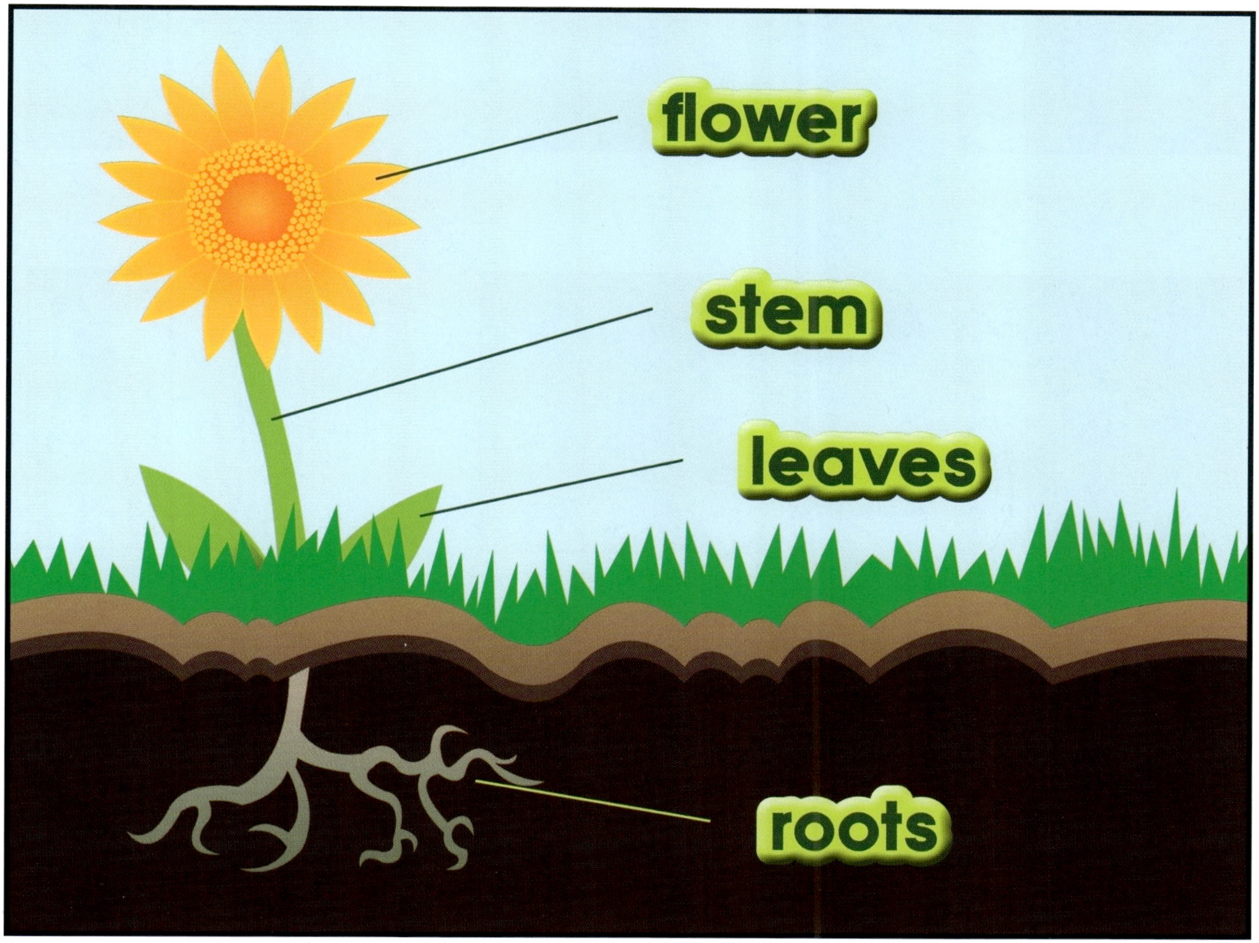

Words to Know

flowers

fruit

leaves

roots

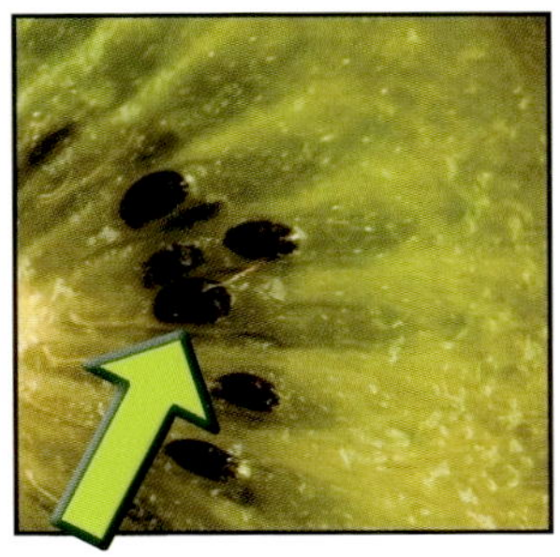

seeds

stems

Index

ROSEN
COMMON CORE
READERS

COMMON CORE STATE STANDARDS FOR LANGUAGE ARTS (CCSS-LA)

Reading: Informational Text

RI.K.4. With prompting and support, ask and answer questions about unknown words in a text.

Language

L.K.1. Demonstrate command of the conventions of standard English grammar and usage when writing or speaking.

- Use the most frequently occurring prepositions.

Rosen Classroom™

ISBN: 978-1-4488-8725-5
6-pack ISBN: 978-1-4488-8726-2
9 781448 887255

C

Weather Watchers
HOT
E.C. Andrews

Weather Watchers

I0807239

HOT

WRITTEN BY
E.C. Andrews

KidHaven
PUBLISHING

Published in 2025 by
KidHaven Publishing, an Imprint of
Greenhaven Publishing, LLC
2544 Clinton St., Buffalo, NY 14224

© 2024 BookLife Publishing Ltd.

Written by: E.C. Andrews
Edited by: Rebecca Phillips-Bartlett
Designed by: Jasmine Pointer

All facts, statistics, web addresses and URLs in this book were verified as valid and accurate at time of writing. No responsibility for any changes to external websites or references can be accepted by either the author or publisher.

Cataloging-in-Publication Data

Names: Andrews, E.C.
Title: Hot / E.C. Andrews.
Description: Buffalo, New York : KidHaven Publishing, 2025. | Series: Weather watchers | Includes glossary and index.
Identifiers: ISBN 9781534547377 (pbk.) | ISBN 9781534547384 (library bound) | ISBN 9781534547391 (ebook)
Subjects: LCSH: Heat--Juvenile literature. | Temperature--Juvenile literature. | Weather--Juvenile literature.
Classification: LCC QC981.3 A537 2025 | DDC 551.5'25--dc23

All rights reserved.
No part of this book may be reproduced in any form without permission in writing from the publisher, except by a reviewer.

Manufactured in the United States of America

CPSIA compliance information: Batch #CSKH25
For further information contact Greenhaven Publishing LLC at 1-844-317-7404.

Please visit our website, www.greenhavenpublishing.com.
For a free color catalog of all our high-quality books, call toll free 1-844-317-7404 or fax 1-844-317-7405.

Find us on

IMAGE CREDITS

All images are courtesy of Shutterstock.com, unless otherwise specified. With thanks to Getty Images, Thinkstock Photo and iStockphoto.
Cover – Andrey Bocharov, Ed Connor, Tomas Ragina, aappp, PrasongTakham, Andrew Rybalko, Ponomus. Character – Andrew Rybalko. 2–3 – ShineTerra. 4–5 – FOTOGRIN, A3pfamily, Guenter Albers, Ponomus. 6–7 – M.Aurelius, Sunny studio, New Africa, Marish, Jane Kelly. 8–9 – Tatevosian Yana, Vectorfair, LeManna, Net Vector. 10–11 – HTeam, fizkes, Maria Maheras. 12–13 – Eryx V, Billion Photos, solomon7, Ponomus. 14–15 – Littlekidmoment, Hakase_420, Kolonko, AlexanderTrou, Leremy. 16–17 – Teri Virbickis, Samuel Borges Photography, inspiring.team, NYS. 18–19 – New Africa, leolintang, Pyty, Valentina Vectors. 20–21 – Christian Roberts-Olsen, i am adventure, Maike Hildebrandt. 22–23 – Sergey Novikov, anastasiya parfenyuk, irin-k.

CONTENTS

Words that look like **this** can be found in the glossary on page 24.

WHAT IS WEATHER?

Welcome to Weather Watchers TV. My name is Dawn and I will be your weather forecaster for today. Before we begin, let's talk about what the weather actually is.

Weather is what you can see and feel in the air outside. There are many different kinds of weather. It can be rainy, windy, snowy, or sunny. Today, we're talking about hot weather.

HOT WEATHER

Summer is the time of year when the sun is closest to us. This brings longer days and warmer weather.

Summer is the hottest season of the year. I always look forward to the sunny days. Spending a bit of time in the sunshine is good for you and can make you feel happier.

FUN IN THE SUN

Hot weather can be lots of fun. You can go to the beach and build sandcastles. Have fun, but be careful, all you sun-loving beachgoers. Make sure you do not get a sunburn!

Make sure you wear sunscreen to protect your skin from sunburn. When you wear sunscreen, it is best to put more on every two hours. Remember to put sunscreen on before and after going swimming.

SUN SAFETY

Wearing a sun hat in the hot sunshine will help protect your head from sunburn. Adding a snazzy pair of sunglasses will protect your eyes and the skin around them.

Drinking plenty of water is another great way to stay healthy in the sunshine. Water keeps your body hydrated. You could try setting up a hydration station at school or at home.

SWEAT

When the weather is hot, you might notice that you sweat a lot more than usual. This is totally normal. In fact, it happens for a reason. So, how does it help?

A layer of sweat helps to cool down your skin. When your skin cools down, your body temperature gets lower. And so, the hotter the weather, the more you sweat!

LOOK OUT FOR HEATSTROKE

Being in hot temperatures for too long can cause heatstroke. This happens when you get too hot for your body to control. Heatstroke can make you feel sick, dizzy, and confused.

Heatstroke can make you very sick, so it is important to follow sun safety tips. If you or your friend start feeling ill in the heat, move to a shady spot and tell a grown-up.

Turn to page 10 for my top sun safety tips.

SUMMER SNACKS

Frozen fruit bars are a great snack for sunny days. Blend up some of your favorite fruit, throw in a Popsicle stick, and pop them in the freezer overnight. They are super easy to make!

Other tasty summer snacks include watermelon, cucumber, and cold salads. Summer fruits like cherries, peaches, and mangos are delicious and nutritious. They will help you feel refreshed and keep you hydrated.

HEAT WAVES

A heat wave is when the weather becomes hotter than usual. Sometimes it can get so hot that it becomes unsafe for people to live in.

Heat waves last for at least three days, but they are often longer. Some heat waves have lasted many months. One of the longest heat waves in the world was in China. It lasted over two months.

HEATED DISASTERS

Heat waves can affect how things work around you. Hot, dry weather makes it easier for things to catch fire in certain places. Heat waves can cause terrible fires in forested areas.

Heat waves can also cause droughts. A drought is when there isn't enough rain for a long time. This can cause water shortages. Animals don't have enough to drink, plants die, and farmers can't grow crops.

SAFE SUMMER

It was shaping up to be a scorcher, and a scorcher it was! Summer is a great time of year, but it is important to take care of yourself and others.

When summer comes along, make sure you have refreshing food, water, and sun hats at the ready. And don't forget your sunscreen!

I am Dawn and this has been Weather Watchers TV. Thanks for tuning in. We will see you next time.

GLOSSARY

CROPS plants that are grown on a large scale to be eaten or used

HYDRATED to have enough water for the body to work

NUTRITIOUS contain lots of natural things that plants and animals need to grow and stay healthy

SHADY sheltered from the sun

SHORTAGE when there is not enough of something

SUNBURN when skin gets burned after being in the sunshine for too long

TEMPERATURE how hot or cold something is

INDEX